Musings

A Collection of Written Words
Short stories, Musings, Poetry
and more

By: Charles Lightwalker

MAPLE
PUBLISHERS

Musings

Author: Charles Lightwalker

Copyright © 2024 Charles Lightwalker

The right of Charles Lightwalker to be identified as author of this work has been asserted by the author in accordance with section 77 and 78 of the Copyright, Designs and Patents Act 1988.

First Published in 2024

ISBN 978-1-83538-315-5 (Paperback)

Cover design by: River Lasol

Book layout by:
White Magic Studios
www.whitemagicstudios.co.uk

Published by:
Maple Publishers
Fairbourne Drive, Atterbury,
Milton Keynes,
MK10 9RG, UK
www.maplepublishers.com

A CIP catalogue record for this title is available from the British Library.

All rights reserved. No part of this book may be reproduced or translated in any form or by any means, electronic or mechanical, including photocopying, recording or by any information storage and retrieval system without written permission from the author.

This book is a memoir. It reflects the author's recollections of experiences over time. Some names and characteristics have been changed, some events have been compressed, and some dialogues have been recreated, and the Publisher hereby disclaims any responsibility for them.

Contents

Introduction 7
Dedication 8
Forward 9
Blind 10
One more chance 11
A Woman's Starlight 12
Musical Woman 13
A Part 14
Past relationship 15
Free 16
Escape 17
Join Hands United Stand 18
Random Thoughts 19
Saturday, January 17, 1981 20
Indulgent self 21
Poet? 22
Out of Place 23
Social Lunch 24
Ukiah February 28, 1979 25
The Moment of Release 26
Whirlwinds of change 27
Rain, rain, it pours on down! 28
Dr. Dale 29
Egocentric 30
21 Illusions 31
Flowering 32
Forest Mother 33
Burning Bridges 34
Wisp of Woman - For Shadow light 35
Lady Lori 36
Jumbled Thoughts 37

God- Dog-God	38
Lady maiden	39
Changes	40
Middle age Spread	41
Bankers Thoughts	42
J.L.	43
Mississippi Mudflats	44
Thank you	45
After Thoughts	46
Section 2, Short Stories, musing, poetry and more	47
The Equation	48
Sailing along with Captain Magic	49
Stories in the Mind!	51
Memory Bank 1974	53
Rambling On	54
Super Short Story	56
A Flash in Life	57
Questions, Quotations, Quills	60
Present Space	61
Question: Can reality exist?	62
Marcus Magic	63
Brother Harry	64
Alice Lema"s Light	65
A Poem for Forever	66
Earth School	67
Joni's joy	69
Natures Person	70
Yoyo Dee Buddha	71
Friendship	72
Fantasy's scenes	73
Forest Site	74
Ego Poem	75
WIFE	76
Sweet Remembrance	77
Time Control	78
	Just Me

Iron Mother	80
Summer Court Or Springs delusion	81
=Suspense	82
Ramblings	83
My Revolution-My Revelation	85
Reworded	86
Magic Moments	87
Listening to Spirit	88
Rebel	89
Love Ya!	90
Children	91
Freda	92
Golden Arches	93
Whirl Winds of Change	94
Once	95
Sweet Remembrance	96
Inspiration of A Lost Generation	97
WHIP FLASH SOUP INTRODUCTION	98
BERKLEY 1973	99
GOLDEN CHARIOT	100
SHIRLEY ANN	101
APPLE TREE	102
MADNESS	103
74 REVOLUTIONS PER MINUTE	104
SPIRITUAL RELEASE	105
BUBBLE	106
COBWEB	107
MOUNTAIN THOUGHT	108
10 MINUTES FROM NOWHERE	109
THE ILLUSIONS OF THE WORLD	110
TRANQUILITY	111
SINSEMILLA ROCKS MY SOUL	112
STONED	113
GARDEN	114
THE ROOM	115
PASSING BY	116
40 STEPS TO THE LEFT	117

ONE DAY IN MY LIFE	118
PRIMAL MADNESS	119
WILLIAM TELL OVERTURE	120
RIDICULOUS	121
BULLSHIT	122
MY	123
MARY SUE AND CINDY TOO	124
LOVE YA	125
RADICAL REALIZATIONS	126
BLACK RYE	128
SWING SLOWLY	129
AFTER THE MORNING	130
MOMENTS NOTICE	131
WOMEN	132
SUDDENLY	133
TOGETHER	134
ONE DAY IN 74	135
BLISS IS BEFORE ME	136
REALITY	137
ANSWER ME	138
UNNOTICED	139
G.I. BLUES	140
NO NAME	141
KATHLEEN	142
FRIENDSHIP	143
COURTROOM DRAMA	144
MIDDLE AGE SPREAD	145
TIME CONTROL Remembered	146
WOW!	147
BOOGIE	148
EACH DAY	149
RAINY MAY DAY	150
SEATTLE SCENE 22	151
Afterthoughts- Ending Musings	152
Dad Day 22	155
Child of Rhyme	156
Friendship	157

Introduction

This second collection of poetry, thoughts, and words was begun during the finishing of 4th Dimensional Space revolution. These pages take you through several periods in my personal life, ups and downs, joy and sorrow. I hope you reflect upon these pages and see between the lines, as well as the lines themselves.

Each of the following pages reflect the inner thoughts and feelings of myself. The ego, Narcissus & selfless service pass through me as only a channel, a part of the cosmic circus. My act is to perform endless illusions, manifestations, interlaced with reality. As a poet, philosopher, magician and master of words and symbols. A clear light, unconditioned, uncontrolled, flowing endlessly across the paper.

Troubled times have already begun. The revolution is slowly progressing. May the new age shine light upon all of us.

Mid-Mountain/winter morning, Mendocino County California

This original introduction was written in 1976, and now I am finally getting around to publishing these written words, 2022, a lot has changed since these poems and written words were written, yet much I have felt during this time is still within me. - Charles-Spokane, Washington February 2022

The revolution is still progressing forward, more in my own mind than in the community, although there is change occurring.

Dedication

To the God in all of us

(This dedication was written in 1976)

And now the dedication from 2022

To the God that exists within each of us!

Forward

This forward was first written in 1991

These writings, from 1976 through 1990 come from a period of growth and change in my life. Lots of changes from a mountain man poet from the homestead movement into a new wave/ activist-social welfare worker. During this time, I experienced a spiritual awakening of the darkness and the light. It was a time to look within the man Charles. I am a member of the baby boomer generation, a radical child of the 60's. A man in his midlife change becoming an adult man who accepts his child spirit. A man coming to terms with his roots, his beliefs, his fears, his strengths and his weakness.

These writings were inspirational memories of the thoughts and psychic energy patterns traveling through my brain. Perhaps these writings were parts of the whole, aspects of the various parts that are me, the lifetimes lived before, the souls of the dead who at times possessed me and tried to live through me. Now as I write this forward to my past writings, I write of another me, another time, another chapter in my life.

The collection of writings composed in this book is a map of my insanity, my mind at various stages of evolution, of a child growing into an adult. From my early twenties through my thirties into my forties, these writings were emotional inspirations, spiritual insights, foolish dreams and fantasies. Ups, downs and some in-between.

They were written during a span of time that is but a moment in my memory bank, a times of many loves and sorrows. This collection is my past. Fall/Autumn 1991 Willow Creek California.

Blind

My insight was unseen in the realm of darkness,

Like a black Rider at Midnight on a moonless night.

My mind galloping along in illusion, falsehoods, and fantasy. Unaware that reality is masked in confusion,

Uncentered on this world in front of it!

Shock waves flash across the screen of the mind

Alerting it to the blurred vision of happiness.

Like LSD, an altered state of consciousness is reached, Opening the floodgates of rational thought

Flowing over a waterfall of memories and social conditioning.

With new eyes we see the world as the multidimensional time

Space continuum it is!

A flowing light energy of crystal-clear rainbow colors circling in radiated fashion.

One more chance

Just one more chance.

I must apologize

For all the things I've done>

Songs of you pass through my mind

For confession, to my obsession for love! Spiritual Heaven! Life! Freedom from Babylon! Free!

Entering my second childhood!

A rebirth of the wildness within me, my spirit. A reawakening of the soul,

The 60's adventure of the mind!

Moments of flashed of you and I

As Fleetwood Mac plays "Say that you love me"

Dancing to the beat, Floating to the rhythm, Sailing with the lyrics, Lost within the dream.

Memories, memories, of my youth and times past.

A Woman's Starlight

I know a woman named Angelina

Who is as beautiful as her name does sound?

She's like a rare and precious gem that is hardly ever found

And when she smiles at me, it set the world on fire! And fills me with emotions and desire!

So I write this poem just for you.

Because you fill my mind with love and life, Someday I pray

You'll be my wife.

Then all our troubles will melt away, just like the loneliness of

Yesterday.

Musical Woman

She's Country Western Feet!

Can chatter jazz and soul through her teeth!

Has a rock n Roll heart but hears a Reggae beat!

She's a musical woman who's got rhythm and blues

With classical fingers playing a treat!

A Part

Although we are apart,

Separated by the system's rules.

Our love is beyond all boundaries

Of the system's fools.

No one can match the clever mind

and our meditative tools.

In distant worlds, we will meet

As water flows into Pools.

Our hearts will beat as one in time

Forever waiting for you in my mind.

Past relationship

Sometimes I think of you

Remembering the good,

Trying to forget the sad!

Wishing it had been different,

That we were still like one!

Skipping though the grass,

hand in hand laughing together

with dreams of a life in happiness.

But the nightmare still haunts me,

The separation of our souls,

The games between us,

The games within us,

the games that others played upon us.

The nightmare comes and goes,

Haunting memories of our relationship,

Of all the trouble we went through,

Of all the hurt we went through,

Of all the pain we went through,

Of all the times we went though.

Free

To create the mindset of the true self,

The inspirational energy must be free to express itself

Free to flow forth with the hidden light of God.

The life force energy which encompassed

In the DNA cells of all humans, animals and plants.

My inspirational side is written words,

Flowing endlessly on a page,

Like water drops sliding down a flower petal

Words are expressions of the inner self,

The left brain, the white light of purity.

Escape

To escape into peace,

Into the jungle of trees and shrubs.

To gaze upon the waterfall of tranquility.

To find peace within oneself so one may step back

Into the world of people with peaceful thoughts

And actions.

For in the inner peace of the mind

Is the peace of the world.

Charles June 1991

Join Hands United Stand

Join hands and form a circle!

Gather round, gather round.

All God's people living on the land!

To think prejudice still exists in the dawning of a new age. My cabin is

ready to circle. If united we must stand again, then let's join hands, one and all!

stand up for Spaceship earth is full of God's people – that means all of us!

To think prejudice still exists, in the dawning of a new age! My cabin's

ready to circle. If you/united we must stand, then let's all join hands on and all Stand Up!

For spaceship earth is full of all God's people, that means all of us!

If United we must Stand

Then let's all join hands,

one and all stand Up!

Join hands and form the circle

Gather round, gather round, join hands

For United we Stand!

This poem was written while attending the forming of a group to be

called United Stand, to fight the housing injustice being imposed upon

us by the county of Mendocino, California.

Random Thoughts

Saturday morning, 2 am Rain pours upon the roof, beating patterns of joy, the drought parched earth soaks up the droplets like a sponge

The drenching rain slides quickly over the heard ground seeking cracks

and crevices

Cloud pass overhead dropping more needed rain

you can hear the earth delight in quenching it's thrist!

Mother nature in her awesome display of control the symbolic healing

Earth in heaven

When the clouds touch the ground-sky and earth meet!

In God's dance of delight sharing,

The balance of light and dark

Rain like winter a cycle in time

It is 2;30 am the candle flickers in the darkness surrounding me, as the raindrops gently beat upon my roof in a majestic tranquility, suddenly a spot in the storm- Rain dripping off the roof. Again, the rain begins it pattern of rhythmic beats above my head as I write.

January 17,1981 Mendocino, California

Praise God, Allah, Jesus, Krishna, Buddha, Da Free John, Lee Me , you, Us

Saturday, January 17, 1981

2:45 am

Wide Awake still trying to sort it all out

Up and down- yin and yang

Dreams-fantasy-reality

Blending my many parts together into a productive whole,

Serving God, the spirit of love, understanding my racing,

Calculating mind, ego -self

The existence of the physical body is real

On stage , star performance, curtain ending- death!

Around the corner death always exists over your shoulder face death, it

awaits us all, like a stranger waiting yet we are the creators of our "own" destiny.

John Lennon was a musical saint, come to play God's tunes

Give peace a chance, follow in love

Become a dreamer, look within, Reflect!

Starting over is the key, unlock the door to your heart!

Let the world be as one, In spirit! In Heart!

Death is life, Life is death, Illusions are mirrors,

Reflections of our soul

Indulgent self

Pig out, stuffing yourself on desire.

Spacing out, stuffing yourself on nothing

Junking out,

overloading the system with Inorganic -plastic -chemical matter

Sugar fix, shooting the body with sweet, Sugar, sugar, sugar

Ego centering Ego Centering- Ego Centering

Nothing means anything, why does anything have to mean something? Survival-existence

Meaning less cultural symbols

Destroy individuality

Create inhuman computerized zombies!

We are all dead, life is a dream!

Heaven is hell, Balance-Yin and Yang

Right- left

What does it all mean?

Nothing!

Poet?

Poetry is but words,

Of a fleeting moment in time

A poet is an illusion,

As false as her words.

The poem itself,

Riddled with grammar

Lines real straight.

Out of Place

Vegetarianism is a strange dis ease!

Meat and potatoes and still the scene!

Karmic law doesn't hesitate! Fate!

When people line the cattle stalls,

Slaughters fine,

Thick and thin

People steaks

Will soon be In!

Social Lunch

Time patterns within the little café,

Coming – going

The sharp noise of the fire truck,

Breaks the stillness, but only for a moment

Social chatting, smoke pollution,

Tables filled with trash!

Clean sweep, all is new-table clear

A sudden change

Reality Altered

Waiting,

Thoughts drifting,

Emotions hanging

Self reflection,

Dreaming eyes – distance stares

Lost in space,

Questions, unanswered

Turning within-turning without.

Ukiah February 28, 1979

Emotional upheaval, waiting stress

Excitement entranced, confusion decision

Rainy drops of fear

Drip endlessly from the sky

Loneliness,

Looms overhead, Like a cloud

*

Warmth, glowing brightly

Within the heart

Melting years of long Unhappiness

Bringing forth youthful sparks of Joy!

Rebirth, Reenergized, Review, Relive, Reflect

Cosmic crystal-clear sunshine, bursting forward

Lighting the sky, heavens, beyond!

The Moment of Release

Energy charges of class action

Different vibrational experiences

Sociological scramble

Value readjustment- set patterns

Cool clean

Clear emotion

Bursting fragments of pent-up energy

Climaxing into

A dreamless void

Of self-relief.

Mendocino County February 7, 1979

Whirlwinds of change

In the mist of change

Everything in motion

Standing still

In the center of

Time!

Overlooking the infinite

Wholeness

Floating endlessly in

pace warp

Cracks

Beneath my feet

Cement shifting with age!

January 8, 1981

Rain, rain, it pours on down!

Rain, rain, it pours on down!

Snow. It drifts and floats around!

(Winter times familiar sound)

A watershed of ups and downs!

Sun shine brakes it

Water erodes the ground

Ice melts, water flows,

Rivers start,

Lakes begin,

Oceans fill to the wind!

Clouds arise- the ocean mist.

A cosmic guide

Of future twist!

Dr. Dale

Dr. dale the night tripper, is rocking on down, guitar in hand

He's got soul, his fingers playing rock n roll

The guitar sings

The baseman swings

Country western

Or

The punk scene

Music his life- his dreams

A Leap year child when he was born

Pieces float through the storm

Both directions

And none are wrong

Egocentric

My poetry

is

Pleasure

My poetry

Is

Great

Simply

Because

I

Wrote

It!

I do not write for people

I write for me!

21 Illusions

A poem I write,

Just for Su!

Full of words and letter

My thoughts to You!

May this day shine

Crystal blue!

If silence speaks

Love to you.

A poem I write just for You

Full of words and letters

My thought to you

May the day shine

Like the light within you

If silence speaks

Let it ring out loud

Love for You!

The birthday wish

I confess

Written words are a mess

But deep within my soul I hold a silent wish for you eternal happiness

Flowering

A poem about Lynn, bookkeeper

For the Herbicide Task Force

New friend

Lynn a friendly female

A girl so sweet!

But heavenly woman from head to feet

A mind of sense and balance sheets

Volunteer time on her own treat!

Community giving from heart and soul

Lynn's beauty does,

Unfold

Reveal the person I behold!

The dance of life does complete

Blooming essence

Of your receipt!

July 3, 1984

Forest Mother

Poem about Caroline and beautiful son, Forest-

Friends, Golden princess,

Songwriter, singer,

Performer, Woman

Caroline, sweet Caroline

With forest delight!

Mother's visions, child's television

Love and hate so intermixed

With former husband dirty tricks

Mother's love, and son's confusion

Dreams, reality and visions

So many paths in all directions!

Which one leads to perfection?

With God's grace,

And golden heait in lace

So divine spirit, unite your soul

Caroline reborn one day!

Light shine, the God's I pray!

Sing your way to the conclusion, breakaway illusion, Spirit strength

Caroline, Caroline, Caroline. July 3, 1984

Burning Bridges

A poem about Sharleen, after having a conversation with Rob &
Sharleen on the past. Paradise Ridge Café. July 3, 1984

Cut the cord of our existence

Separate dreams an illusion!

Face the facts

Without confusion!

End the tie, that binds my spell!

So, a broken heart can be well!

Like the paths that now does fork in different directions!

Our lives are separate

Each seeking its own perfection!

Although a joy we once had

Made us friends I am glad!

Burn the bridges of our past

make the moment

forever fast.

Wisp of Woman - For Shadow light

Written about Sharleen S (January 5, 1981)

Sharleen was she a mist?

Sharlene's the phantom of my soul inner mercy- mother grace

Was she a dream?

Sharleen so lovely, sweet kind

illusion fantasy of my mind

Sharlene the mother, warm and true

Loves her children four times told

Hanging high swing low

Questions- Answers- things untold!

Is she real is she fate?

like a mirror- open face

Yin and Yang life

Responsibilities, hell and hate

Loves and balance, recreate

Meeting her was my fate!

Lady Lori

The presence of a woman

In all her delight!

A mother of children

With grace and insight

A person she be it,

A lady by right!

Her beauty astounding

A glorious sight!

May god grant surrender

Wisdom that Might!

May this woman and I be one tonight!

Jumbled Thoughts

Dreams of an ending

past and present blending

new family roots are growing

conscious evolutionary growth

Parenthood reality

Stereotype images

Bold new adventure

Life unending

Drama!

God- Dog-God

I am the gentleness of a breeze

Upon your face

I am the rhythmic sound of love

Pounding in your heart

I am the grace of God

Standing before you!

I am all things unto you

The mirror reflecting

Upon you!

Lady maiden

So fair,

So true,

Hearts of love,

Miles apart

Spirit- One

United Hearts!

Mother image- gentle kind

Two children grace divine

Loving tender

Division arts

Illusion mirrors

Truth in our hearts!

One way street

Exit

Do Not Enter

Trespassing

One way street

Wrong Way

Watch out

Scam Sham

Dandy Ego

Changes

I watch the world twisting

Love and life around.

I'm listening to the people

Just waiting for a friendly sound

Though my eyes I see many don't care

Sometimes I wonder if anyone's ever sincere

Am I looking at it wrong, do you suppose?

Life's a gamble, you never really know

I see the pieces going together

If se all try, it might get better

People change so much, it really blows my mind

Life a gamble you never really know

I turn my head the other way

Though my eyes I watch life's play

Sometimes I wonder if it all makes sense

Once you're in, you're out again

Life's a gamble. I don't know.

What can I say I want to fly away.

Middle age Spread

40 frustrations with aging time!

Middle age spread!

Balding grey spots

On surfer images and hippy dream!

Aging radical with capitalists' seams

Wearing suits of corruption for pensions extremes!

Bankers Thoughts

I grab upon material pleasures

And find them meaningless.

I search among my friends

And find many who are not.

I look upon the greatness of man

And find the beast of an animal.

I learn the system is a game

And find me the loser.

This poem was written while I was working for Bank of America as a Student relations representative while attending Canada Community College.

J.L.

An artist

Fair and true

A sculpting hand

Carving a new.

A heart of an artist through and through

This poem was written about an artist -sculptor friend and drinking buddy. We attended Canada community college together in Redwood City, California. 1971

Mississippi Mudflats

To see me is not to understand

me.

To know me is to hope to understand

Me.

To be my friend is to be a part of

Me.

To gently float down the Mississippi mudflats of life.

Exit

Your eyes are a part of me

Feeling as I do.

I detect a tear of sadness sas you leave with

Part of

Me.

Sweet Sixteen

She lies there as beautiful as a summer morning.

Her voice sings out

the joy of love.

She sees the world with the eyes of innocence.

End

Th poetry you have reads was not written for you, nor money

Fame or glory

But

Simply for the pleasure of writing for that in and of

itself is rewarding enough

Thank you

Thank you, thank you, for sharing your poetry, your feelings.

It made me see that part of myself that's negative, that needs to change.

Thank you, thank you for letting me more clearly see the hurt I caused you,

The pain the suffering.

Thank you, thank you for being such a friend to tell the truth about the hurt inside of me,

The negative vibrations that have sickened me.

Thank you, thank you, and now I can see

I ask your forgiveness,

And I pray the changes come rid all the negativity from me.

I'll think of you with fond thoughts,

And a sadness of what we as a couple could really be.!

After Thoughts

The poetry and writings in this book has been a labor of love, and has been a healing for me as I have gone through the writings of my past, digging deep into my late 20's then into my thirties, and then my

forties, my fifties, midlife, and the changes I was experiencing as I travel on my journey, then I took a break for awhile eventually coming back to writing again in my late sixties, with a spark in seventies to continue to write and publish my written words. This has been an ongoing

discovery of written material I had sorted away in files and boxes. And now that I am reaching a new mile stone of turning seventy -five, I feel it is time again to express myself and to share with the world my feelings as I reach a status as an elder, and to share my adventures of life. I can only hope that this work will reach those that which to understand me and my writing, and the different eras and times I lived. I am hopeful that my daughter will carry on with her writing and will reach the levels of her success, and enjoyment as I have in putting pen to paper and typing the essence of my thought to share with others.

I could not have done this writing without the support of my beloved wife Serena, and the continued support of my daughter Mayah. Also wish to thank my many students who have encouraged me to write to share my thoughts, and to continue to write. I hope to finish putting together my buried manuscripts, and short stories into a readable collection of books that can be shared with anyone dreaming to explore that world of magic, healing, wisdom and just thoughts that pass through the human experience we call life. I would love to hear from you the reader, may you be blessed with the time to read and the time to contemplate.

Section 2, Short Stories, musing, poetry and more

Introduction:

This collection of super short stories and musings was written during a period in my life- 28 years old, just moved to the great outdoors. I was living in my owner-built home on eighty acres of land. It was quiet time in my life, peaceful surroundings. It was also a time for political education-Learning-activism, understanding our system of government better.

And now as I write this introduction, I am amid a new phase in my life. I live closer to town in a beautiful home on a quarter acre of land. Time changes as does my writing style, and now I share with all who read these stories a part of me, my writing between 1970-1980. Charles 1985, Arcata, California

The above introduction written in 1985, and now it is 2022, and publication is finally happening, much has passed , relationships have changed and I am again reaching a new phase in my life, a daughter at Gonzaga University, a loving marriage sustained with love. A time of continued learning and teaching, and reflection. Charles, Spokane, Washington-March 2022.

The Equation

The solution to humankind is to revolt within yourself and truly begin to understand yourself. Only then can we begin to question our place in this universe and how we can survive in harmony with nature without destroying ourselves and the planet we exist on.

One fallacy we must overcome is the idea that we are the superior race on this planet. Wrong. We are only another animal in existence within the universe.

The fact we are really atoms and molecules prove we are energy. All existence is composed of energy. Thus, logically, we could say that if all energy is in harmony with all energy within the universe, then we exist in what we could classify (as some would say, impossible) Utopia.

$Gn + Nn = An + Un = O$

Gn- Energy in Harmony

Nn- Nature which is really energy

An- Harmony of nature and energy, in harmony together

Un- Universe in Harmony

O- upon reaching this level, we will no longer value these words

Sailing along with Captain Magic

The sun slowly sinks behind the pale blue sea, the twilight of time, disappearing into the cool blue sky.

Our adventure begins with the change in time, the moment between the sunlight and starlight. We travel a swift path of flight to reach the outer hole in space, precisely at the moment of creation, bursting through to Galaxies beyond the realm of pure human understanding yet, many tales unfold as we begin our flight in fantasy among starship Mind warp, led by Captain Magic I. Mirror, who travels the realms of inner space , who works for GOD Central, overseer of the planets, Guardian of Knowledge, ride the gentle waves, floating along with the starship Mindwarp . Upon entering the void in space, reality is no longer in logical attunement. All control s is on automatic god control, using technology light years beyond! Black! Crystal memories of past journeys rummage through me. Captain Magic! Hello, lose yourself- release in soul-rock n roll, turn the speakers on, we have broken through to the other side. The air is filled with joyous sounds, Rolling stones, Jefferson starship, Beatles, Kiss, Dylan. Captain Magic all is in front of you! We are now approaching the planet -Quir- lifeforms of the tenth magnitude, stop for refueling-supplies, begin radio contact with Quir high command David Bowie. Prepare for our arrival, thirteen stellar days from now, compute on knowledge in banks- interlock via computer, communications link, monitor or all!

Read back -send message-trip flight pattern not registered, incomplete data, unable to compute, advance problems-inner planet war- all computer links inoperative- radioactive winds-abnormal patterns- suggest travel to Trizone, sixteen stellar days, begin radio contact. Authorize! Authorize! Captain Magic approves alternate plan, begin contact -voiceprint!

Quickly, it all ends, madness-the insanity surfaced. They carried him off

to the loony bin! To use Pins! Code 4.... End broadcast!

Captain Magic Illusion Mirror

*

The planetary reality- survival- illusions

Gods-Temple to Money- Symbolic

We must begin to understand the illusion, the lotus blossom of revolution is flowering. The seed is cast to the wind. The mind becomes clear. Truth! Reality must be seen in its social relationship to all things, Karmic Law, balance, Earth. The path is simple! Simple obvious Reality! Illusions Fade, Appropriate Technology, Yin and Yang, Simple Living Peace. You, Me, One! The Cosmic waves flow endlessly from the void! Silence! A divine fool sits in laughter, a wise man contemplates, ego fantasies, Cosmic Circle, Surrounding. Rat Race!

Zazen frozen. Efficiency of space! Buckminster Fuller, Bubba Free John, Lee Louzawits, Steven Gaskin, Ram Das, Krishna, Kripal Singh, Jerry Brown Jr., Stewart Brand, Wild Willie Weed Seed!

The paradox is unraveling, truth is, grace, energy, the eternal Tao. I am but a circuit, a channel for the flow, words are endless, meaningless silence is!

The dormant kundalini, opens the valve, let it flow, release the Godhead, set loose the primal scream. Relationship with all things, Oneness! Live your Sadhana, the act, your trip, the part inn the puzzle, "Is but a piece of the Action" ! Join in Satsang, Letthe Grace flow! My company is love, my business, selling Nirvana! Enlightenment! Reality! Performing the cosmic circus- a show to disrupt you, corrupt you- an invitation to the dance, a Celebration of Life!

*

I had computerized the entire system, the programming was correct, all logic was illogical- the experiment began precisely on time, the computer analyzed the input data and began processing the information into her memory banks. With each passing moment, the computer's relearning caused complete malfunction of the entire unit. Success! At last, the ultimate weapon-deprogramming a computer- making it functionality useless- inoperable- Plans were set in motion- training would begin- Spies would be trained in the art of malfunction- major computer- Complete havoc would be created by deprogramming major computers throughout the world- Operation Override- security Systems must be completely cut off- Errors could create nuclear accidents- warheads going off- Push the wrong button- All out War- Yet malfunction is complete illogic would shut security systems down, dismantle itself, obsolete-wipe out codes-decode- record- It weas like a giant chess match with each move calculated logically according to normal programming- illogic reversed all trends= God existed in programming: an illogical assumption unproven in present data banks- new programming reorganizes facts illogically God does exist- he is Santa Claus at 1211 Church Street- Megalopolis United Mexican Alliance of South America and Nations-year 1984-

The above was written by a certified paranoid Schizoid who was having hallucinations while smoking mushrooms in the year 1981 of our Lord Jesus Christ- Amen

Stories in the Mind!

Sailing along- The breeze blowing through the trees across the water- gently off the coast of Madagascar- divers are searching for old Spanish dollars. News of Russian Cosmonauts walking on the Mars.

Not far away on a small almost deserted island lives Charmin Leganes, tuning in the tiny transmitter radio- news flashes: the United States

today announced and end to frozen foreign accounts, and the easing of regulations allowing citizens to remove money from their savings accounts. India announces a program to end hunger- A National Fast Week- All who live through it are the chosen ones. English parliament went in to special session today to consider demands to Irish terrorists holding Prince Charles captive- complete secession of Ireland from Britain- Charmin flicks the radio- peace enters the air- the birds singing - the waves splashing against the sandy beach- The world beyond the Island is in turmoil. Charmin meditates- praying for peace. The cosmic soul relaxes in itself- lost in the mirror of illusion- believing he/she escapes the madness surrounding earth- like a karmic blanket- meditation is broken by the entrance of a security robot Ar6- reporting chemical dumping within 30 kilometers of the south eastern section of the island. The vessel is from Holland, its commander a Welshman who is working for Spanish Amalgamates of Sidney, Australia. Its contents are radioactive chemical used in research reactors during the early twenty-first century. Directives as to plan of action – secure ship in magnetic hold- mind probe vessel- eliminate crew members- recompute ship's computer to release the toxic substance near home port and to explore near the ship's homebase- Meditation is resumed in lotus position levitating 5 kilometers off the ground. Endless silence is broken two and a half hours later. Overhead misses of African colonies security system- alter path of missiles within a twenty-five mile airspace- use laser beams.

Meanwhile, the Russians have landed on Mars- reports indicate contact with some life forms- new flash: Russian Invaders seized by alien life forms- charged with illegal entry into Mars stellar systems against intergalactic codes set forth in the 1992 agreement signed by the Milky way Governing Council. The United states has announced the formation of a new department of Peace who principle powers will be the coordination of peace demonstrations through the United states. Adolph Hitler, the third was named Chairman of the new department with Martin Swanneck (former head of the Jewish League) as Deputy Commander. The KKK has taken Missouri and Arkansas. Federal troops have pushed to the mason- Dixon line. The secession of Texas, Arizona and New Mexico into the Combay Collective Government has been hardest hit by drought.- Reports indicate the new government is riding high in the saddle handling the situation. Please be advised this is an emergency broadcast from Central America.

Reverend Jim Jones, the second was resurrected today with the bloodshed of hundreds of women and children in honor of our famous Ganja experience.

The Boat People have taken over central Park calling it Bengali West.

Charmin laughs. He remembers when the Gay coalition took over San Francisco in 1984. Federal troops were brought in to quell the violence and fear gripping the city. The Lesbian Revolutionary forces controlled the water-front-downtown section. How well Charmin remembers the secession of San Francisco from the state of California in 1985, not to soon after to be followed by California dividing itself into four sections, Oregon's succession from the United states in 1986 , Washington 1987. Oregon and Washington to join together to form the coalition of freedom states of earth- 1989- soon to be joined by northern parts of what was Northern California, Humbold and Mendocino Counties. It was a bitter struggle against federal forces at the time. However General Charmin was one of the key factors in the revolutionary new government. By destroying the centralized computer system in Northern California, and the taking over of all communication systems, made it possible to put the federal forces at a disadvantage, having to come in on helicopters over the Sierra Nevada Mountains with the revolutionary forces already with anti-aircraft weapons the glorious fight of the hot war years. The island once again appears in his reality- while his mind was in yesteryears dreaming old dreams.

Eva walks up to the cage unleashing her radiant smile. The tiger comes forward. Charmin slowly turns, watching his daughter play with her pet, repeating all things must be free, release the tiger from its cage. Suddenly she appears like a mist, the goddess mother Sharlene woman, queen of the island, her majestic beauty entrancing. Charmin is spellbound in the divine presence of such grace and beauty.

Newflash: Algerian forces have captured Turkish invaders on its borders. Light years ahead, trouble evades paradise- Love conquers hate-her queen ma – the throne of nature-

How well Charmin remembers the trials, the hunting, searching – Big Brother wanted him, crimes against the empire- the destruction of the Iron Mother, spy in the sky of Big Brother.

The underground missions in the polluted cities of the empire, like a tiger in the concrete jungle with the blue meanies forever looking for you, moving from one place to the next each adventure more complex than before- fighting like when the L.A. Police bring in their psychic squad to capture all revolutionaries within a hundred mile radius.

Peace demonstrations in front of the psychic squad Headquarters in Disneyland. Donald Duck was arrested for socialistic pro- worshipping and Captain Kangaroo was court – marshaled for shooting kids up with junk food- he was sentenced to ninety days in an organic mushroom factory, tasting.

I was a great day. The entire police force was soaked wet by the automated firetrucks, plus the actual pie throwing had happened (which was rare in those days). The Kurt K. Klansmen was hit with a black-eyed soul pie delivered by T.T. Honky of the famed peach tree tribe-

It was a great event. Art in action – political art in motion. However, the empire was not totally caught off guard. Within minutes of the first pie, Gestapo agents began jumping out of helicopters. It was pure hell for at least five minutes- until of course Charmin stole one helicopter and began assaulting all incoming agents, and eventually getting away with the helicopter no less!

Time travels airstreams- it was light years behind us all, Sharlene

Woman, Charmin and the God children surrounded by miles of sandy beach.

*

Memory Bank 1974

The slowly loosening tide danced upon the shore and the dawns early light flickered on the waves.

The thoughtfulness overcomes you as you watch the dancing waves, sitting in the lotus position meditating calmly, floating in time along the waves outwardly towards the open sea in search of itself, in search of the world, in search for its very existence upon this space ship called earth, Western Hemisphere, North American sector, concentration state 40, area 310, sub-section zero.

Suddenly the silence is broken with sound of human existence approaching rapidly, almost military in fashion, with a shiny object on the chest area symbolizing forward motion. Without as much as a single word, thoughts sent a message. I simply number 427681232, rating 3 priority privilege.

He swiftly turns in his footsteps and return the same way he approached. I was compelled to speak verbally in ancient English slang terms to express what at one time called anger. The emotional outburst came from primitive sources within deeply imbedded psychological patterns, which existed in 20th century man.

My mind slips back into meditation. Again, I begin to transcend time. All space exists within one space. Many worlds exist within the same space, at different parallels.

The opposite of us stares at me with the same understanding that it simply is. To question why is meaningless since it is fact. We exchange memory and knowledge until we become one—their mine is my mind, and my mind their mind, no longer separate but one unit.

Suddenly our paths uncross and again he exists 3 elsewhere even as he exists here. Strange—a world built on a single point of philosophical logic, a computerized world incapable of emotional realizations, for where there is logic, there is no emotion, for emotion is illogical.

Boy, I sure would hate to punch the wrong data on the computer card? Logic built on an error would be illogical.

Again my silence is broken, with the sound of sweet music filling the air with purple prism fashion. The sound becomes sharper, changing to an absurb red streaking upon the waves.

The music comes from a wandering TX4768, obviously alone with her music. She does not even seem aware of my presence, continuing to send her music out across the waves in harmony with the sea as though she was part of each wave that fell upon the shore. I watch her glide on my path of vision and disappear into the endless shoreline.

The time had come for me to leave the beauty of the sea, and return to sector twelve, subsection zero area 310 of the concentration camp at which I was assigned.

Another day ended in the life of existence of spaceship earth, computer log noted and recorded.

Rambling On
A series of Discussions on Life

The true cop out is man's ability to believe he is superior in terms created by his own ego, defined from only one point of view.

Relationship to true nature is not conquest but harmonious existence free of unnecessary functions created for the game of money. Corporate policies favor expanded knowledge in fields of interest related to concepts created by corporation brainwashing- via media outlets, psychological reinforcement of belief in self ego centered induivial, Importance only self, game in process of establishing normal convenient for the necessary functions of the existence of the present corporate-military system.

Change is question, each person is aware of only existence of his allowed thoughts, psychological reform system set up as rehabilitation program to change mental structure in alignment with corporate policies.

World peace is the existence of human understanding of existence as non ego self. Natural flow with the universe, upset cosmic balance may restore itself in millions of years, but destruction is certain at man's pace toward "progress."

All of time travels around me like bubbles of oil swirling around me endlessly.

Why is reality so confusing? Money is the general hang-up of society.

Why do we exist if not to exist? Creation of money values causes psychological frustration; creation of evil. Man created evil by the belief in its existence. |The creation of money is a form exchange, an unnecessary function if you exist. We cause all frustrations. Knowledge narcissus. Ego psychological need is unnecessary to existence in harmony with planet earth. The species of human beings will slowly die off because we are killing our race. We have outsmarted ourselves. Enjoy the present now for it exists; tomorrow is a word.

I understand enlightenment (The Word) . I have reached Nirvana! Bliss is before me, but others will allow me nothing of it, even when I am already there! They create frustration for themselves.

We all come from different viewpoints, realities! We all exist within a reality we somewhat create! We choose to live in hell or live in love. Understanding, bliss Utopia.

> Each must seemingly achieve a goal!
> Sense of accomplishment!
> Ego dealt with Narcissism.

All points come from the point of reality, the existence of only the present existing as it always has now! However many shapes and forms.

Living as the existence of you at the present time is simply the awareness of the value which is allowing you to be whatever is at the that moment.

Pure existence creates energy, which is neither bad nor good, until the you creates the positive and the negative, and so, in turn, decides if one is getting bad karma or good karma which is obviously a creation of your own situation which is reality.

People can only deal in terms of materialization, symbols of the facts which is already the fact, reality.

Let's discuss the reason for discussion, which has its basis in communication between more than one induvial in order to be a discussion.

Thus we have at least determined that discussion takes place between more than one person, one point which has no relative value to this discussion.

To get back to discussing the r4eason for discussion, we must first find value in the discussion.

So, is there is value in this discussion, which is discussing the reason for discussion, which has yet to be understood.

Maybe this discussion is full of bull, because the point of the subject has been completely ignored.

In dealing with people, we assume that you are you and I am I. Our first conscious thought is the thought of the self.

Since we believe that we exist, we cause the first problem, by believing that we are separate from others. We exist supposedly in a physical body, but true existence is beyond the physical realm in which we live as human beings. Obviously the reality is then a creation of ourselves we believe we exist in.

Ego is the self in conflict with other egos believing ther is separate existence of other selves.

The simple fact is obvious- that we all exist in reality no matter what reality we exist in! Simple existence is simply enough reason for existence. Therefore, if we all exist with reality, we are all one within that reality.

The enlightenment of man/woman is the simple knowledge that he is existing in reality. Reality is therefore truth, perfect knowledge. Since reality can not be changed, it should be accepted as for what it is. Reality.

Reality- the existence of the experience at that moment in time. Therefore, understand that you always exist in reality which is always

present. Which means you can not escape reality for there is no escape. So accepting reality as it is truth.

Truth is enlightenment.

Enlightenment is only the obvious

Therefore, one can assume that reality is enlightenment of the truth which is always was present- it was obvious.

Super Short Story

A story of reality crosses this path of fantasy. A little boy sings to the cattle in the field, a song of sweet innocence, of love that may never come. Suddenly he stops singing. The noise of a giant airplane polluting the stratosphere obviously flies overhead. With clear, bright blue eyes, he stares into the sky above him, watching with interest, yet with a small understanding of the metal bird has seen before.

With the passing of time, again the cattle slowly head towards the barn at dinner time, the boy singing softly in the background, keenly watching for strays and calves that might wander. Over pastures of green grassy mountains and valleys with only the wind to tag along, he continues to sing.

In the distant valley, a man with a plow, six white horses and an army of frogs. As the distance disappears, the leather like skin shadowed with age appears upon the man plowing, the silver shine from white coats of the horses.

Without warning, all this disappears as though it was never there. It has only been a dream, a fantasy, and acid trip.

A Flash in Life

I walked into the area of the band, which was playing loudly will full energy, making your body move to the flow of the music. I stood still with my body vibrating energy flowing crazily along with the music. Suddenly my mind flashes upon the simpleness of her natural beauty. I cosmically try communicating by flowing pure energy thought toward her across the floor, the tables and the people surrounding the area. A direct bolt hits her softly as it if to say hello with feeling of love in your heart.

Confusion seemed to appear upon her being until slowly a smile appeared, of understanding that seemed to quell the music to a silent level of unawareness.

The energy began to increase until it seemed reality was one within itself and the world was composed of us and everything flowed freely amongst us and all was within us and we were within us as one.

Suddenly the energy is broken by an outside force which seeks attention of his presence within your realm of reality. It is also a flas of energy flowing harshly and swiftly towards it tarket.

As you exchange realities without speaking, only realizing the existence as sperate in itself and yet of feeling of unity offered by each.

The moments then changed to awareness of the music still being punched out on the drums with vigor and energy. As I glance back across the tables, she still exists, although now in a sperate reality unaware of my eyes , shooting energy in all directions, seeking the return of energy.

My mind still floating above the crowd, hanging in space, seeing many realities within many more all within one.

But can I choose to know that to choose is not as real as not to choosing, although some would believe it to be so.

Now to again flash upon anothers thoughts and to begin to move my body from this spot which I seem cemented to as the part of the building itself, another reality.

Slowly I move my legs, with the knees bending slightly with the steps I take.

*

Ending

The collection of short stories are absurdities you have just read are interesting to me to reflect upon. As the author of these written words, I find it hard to reach a point of ending. So much of my work ends, because the energy flow stops My writing collection within are a reflection of positive moments in my life's adventure.

This collection was put together to share moments in my life, a time when I was searching for my inward soul, and studying Zen Buddhism. Now in 1985, the same short stories seem distance of another person. I have changed as time changes every second. None the less these

stories are me and my feelings. Arcata, California. Having tea at Plaza Gourmet. Charles

Now 2022, Spokane, Washington, in my basement office, as I compile this collection of writings, words and poetry.

And now the rest of the collection, compiled and organized in June of 2024, Scotland, United KIngdom.

Musings Part Two: a collection of thought, poetry and short stories

Introduction

This collection of words, thoughts,and stories are a collection of my written material from the early 1970's though 2020. Some of this material comes from the various stages in my life, my late 20's, my 30's, 40's, 50's, 60's,and into the beginning of my 70's. As I am writing this I am looking outside at our beautiful roses. We are living in the village of small seacoast town in norhtern Scotland.writing for me has been a passion since I was a teenager, but became much more when I reached my fifties, and has also increase as I watched my child become a writer. This collection has been a long time coming as it has been a process of reading, rereading, and selecting what written material should me included in this book.Even as I write this, I have already begun to write and collect more poetry, thoughts,observations about life to put together another book. I feel quite fortunate to have the time to write, edit and to get feedback from a few friends to create these books that are reflections of my thoughts, my life and my environment. I also have been rejuvenated to update some of my other books, especially those on holistic and complementary health care. And it has made me want to teach again some of the classes I used to teach in America, several years ago. Somehow moving to Scotland has given me a new look on life, a new adventure to pursue, new thoughts rushing through my head, new words forming ideas, prose, stories, poetry. I also feel fortunate at having the opportunity to work with some other talented writers, perhaps creating new books. Using some of my life's adventures as part of the story.

I have lived a very exciting exciting life, having studied a several Universities, a seminary, apprenticed with several medicine woman and men.I have been an ordained as a new thought minister, served as a chaplain, became a member of the Free Cherokee Nation, served as Chief and Elder of the Wolf clan of the pacific northwest. Taught classes in Medical Intuition, Sound Healing with Tuning Forks, Reiki, Spiritual Healing, and How to Operate a Holistic enterprise, I have written hundreds of articles on health, holistic healing, simple living, and new thought philosophies. My life has been an adventure of allowing Spirit to guide me, of allowing my gifts to come forward and be shared with those around me. Even my experiences in the <u>military has shaped my vision of spiritual life while in the human form. The U.S. Army had an incredible impact on my physical body, my mental health and my emotional makeup</u>.

Questions, Quotations, Quills

Help

Secure

Love

Happiness

Speak truth   tidbit

Semantic

Gossip-Talk

Listen

Lost words   See, hear, feel

Of feelings

Echoing

A

Heartfelt song

Weeping loneliness

Forever!

Marigolds, butterfly

Sweet

Honey

Sugar

Absorbing Pastimes

Present Space

There is no other space than the present space, which encompasses all other spaces, for all space is simply space with no real boundaries other than our mind.

We create the limits in which we exist by first believing there are limits. Mistake number one. Thus accepting this fact creates mistake number two- accepting a fact which is not a fact but believing an assumption.

Therefore, the assumption is an error, is the process of the mental thought process.

***

Question: Can reality exist?

Answer: Which reality do you mean? Perhaps there is no reality at all. This assumption that there is, is from your point of reference.

Question: Was my question reality or the simple mistake of assuming that reality exists for me in my mind?

* *

Reality is the beginning of the end.

It encompasses everything.

**

Circle the surrounding elements of time, energy and environment—creation of space, of Reality.

All value has no value for value is a creation of man/woman which believes value is what it is because he/she has said it is.

So value has no value other than value.

Marcus Magic

The silver wolf at his side,

Marcus has circled through time,

Born renewed.

With strength and energy on the move,

To Texas river, Sedona moons, and

Celestial landscapes beyond Neptune.

The thirst for knowledge has led him through

Mystic records and ancient rites

To modern science and computer tools.

His path is forward, to share with you,

His love unfolding from his view.

Charles March 23, 1995

*

Brother Harry

Spaceships landing in a field of dreams,

Alien visitors care, it seems,

With Brother Harry's helpful teams,

To bring together one and all in building future scenes

Of love and harmony in the survival of our genes.

To reach the sky and meet other worldly beings,

Just look within to find the means.

Charles 1995, Twisp, Washington

*

Alice Lema"s Light

A bright young flower blossoming anew,

With Ummat's energy shining through.

Fighting the method of the divine,

To unleash herself in growth and change.

The seed of love implanted deep.

With shakti energy it does seep,

To claim the essence of endless time,

In cosmic swirls of crystal light,

Her unfolding not yet complete,

As the path she walks is an endless street,

As a forest wide of rainbow dreams

That sparkle at each step she takes,

For now it is the time to awake.

*

A Poem for Forever

Johnny Forever

Is a spiritual warrior

Walking a path of delight,

Helping others

By serving them right, loving from heart center's

Chakra bright,

Filling the Methow Valley

With karmic sperities,

Dancing in the eternal

Flame of Light!

Johnny Forever

Is all right!

*

Earth School

The greed-driven failures of the past,

Unfolding for future generations to undo,

A repairing of the planet step by step,

Ecosystem by ecosystem,

A rebuilding of the Garden of Eden

For all of God's children to enjoy.

2/20/1995

Ummati's Scene

A shakti of universal beams,

Of kundalini rising from Earth Mother's

Cosmic streams,

Like a mist of vapor floating

In Father Sky's astral schemes.

The white light of understanding

Reaches deep into your dream,

Bringing God's delight and love serene.

*

Releasing moments of future thought!

Swallowed pride,

Broken heart

Time between—years apart

Seven years of time

To taste

Love is splendor

Ours is fate

Always near—yet far away

Ocean view,

Forest lot

Things will change

Minds and heart

Love is true

Words are not

Touch my soul—you are free

Karmic visions,

Spiritual rot!

The divisions lie in your mind,

Not our hearts

No matter where

Our spirits never part!

*

Joni's joy

Like an adult she does seem,

But her twinkling eyes childlike gleam,

Of a world unfolding in spiritual scenes.

Taking each day as Now

And flowing along in the truest sense

With her path unfolding in rapid sequence.

Like a stream that is flowing

And suddenly falls into song. A waterfall of insight

Bubbling into the pond of life.

With ripples and sounds of delight,

Joni swimming in Ummati's light.

*

Natures Person

Shaula is a nature person,

Wildness surrounds.

A jungle of life shining brightly for she,

The goddess of spirit in bodily clothes,

Floating through space in dance with the flow,

Like a river that's calm and gentle in song.

Shaula is rolling and drifting along,

White light glowing through the trees at dawn.

A forest of feeling, of human dimension,

Singing the love of the heart's intervention.

*

Yoyo Dee Buddha

Upon the road you did appear,

A sitting Buddha of dog delight.

As snow falling in the dark of night,

You jump aboard our truck with might,

And captured the heart of Tara's insight.

With cuteness beyond compare,

And a shivering body of fright,

We took you into our home late that night

To bundle up with care and warm firelight

To join our family in love and light.

You bark your song of canine sprite

And fill our days with endless love and joy.

As you walk on hind legs dancing

With two little feet and shining oh so bright!

*

Friendship

A poem of friendships' might

To reach the heavens, as spirits unite,

Across the waters, a sky so bright,

Filled with love and delight.

For friendships form from golden light

And hearts that open to the night

To share the mysteries of each other's right

To walk the path of God's delight

Make friendship special in my sight.

*

Fantasy's scenes

Your body is transfixed in my mind

With fantasy thought that races through time,

Interdimensionaly wrapped in design

A dream of desire that the heart is aware

Of floating thought of adventure in life

With paths that crisscross a forest of delight.

The fantasy ends, just like the dream,

Amidst the timeless scene.

*

Forest Site

The wind that weeps

With rain falling at your feet.

The silence of snow as it gently falls

From the sky in white sheets.

The sun is shining orange and bright

Peeking through the mountains

At morning's first light,

Filling the shadows of past nights,

With a glimmer of hope and God's delight.

A new day is coming straight at your sight.

Your eyes are waking to live it right.

Another day to walk in the light.

*

Ego Poem

Give everything up to promote Me,

Myself, Charles

Charles Lightwalker,

Writer, poet, dreamer, scientist, and more

Open up Charles to the world—spread his thoughts, ideas!

The message of life—its constant struggle against itself!

I am an illusionary

Master of words.

Creating worlds upon worlds on paper—

Communicating with the joyous love, with Charles.

Each stroke of the pen is another line in time,

Loosening another brick in the wall

Each line of words is part of the whole!

All interconnect- innerlocked

*

WIFE

For you I do write a loving

Poem for my wife,

Who stands beside me,

When I'm ill at ease

And comforts me

With warmth and love Who is One with me United in ecstasy

And separate from the illusion of reality. Who is wife in life

Traveling in the light

And filling all the darkness

With white light.

This is the woman who is my wife, traveling along with me day and night.

*

Sweet Remembrance

Thoughts of you enter my mind

Like crystal clear

Raindrops

Developing into

A pool of beauty

An

Ocean of love

Tranquil

And silent

*

Time Control

Within these hallowed halls of justice

We prepare the motion mix

To play the legal game in action!

Time sits still in all its glory,

Suspended by the judge's order,

Fix the time and the date

To reappear, before the bench

Lawyers, Judges and the Clerks

Work in details and perfection

but final say can be rendered

Only by code books silent

Surrender—accept the fate

Of rules and regulations,

Society's answer.

*

Just Me

Nobody sees what I can see

For back of my eyes there

Is only me

And nobody knows how my

Thoughts begin

For there's only me

Inside my skin.

Isn't it strange how

Everyone owns

Just enough skin to

Cover their bones?

My father's would be too big for me to fit in

I would be all wrinkled inside of it.

And my baby brother's is way too small

It wouldn't cover me up at all

But I feel just right

In the skin I wear

And there's nobody like me

Anywhere.

Iron Mother

Corporate fools

Military fate

Iron Mother child of Big Brother

Flying overhead

Wind-chopping

Iron blades

Circle round the underfed!

Flying over not the rich man's land

Search among the poor instead

Metal machine

Computer fed

Keep in line, keep it straight!

Iron mother Big Brother say

Love is Hate!

Summer Court Or Springs delusion

First day of summer
It does unfold!
The courtroom drama
A legal web untold!
Decision final
And the Judgment set!
Release from tension
And overall threat!

A judge decides my fate today
By reading facts or
perhaps confusion
I wish that all I see be
but a dream and I awake
From these illusions!

=Suspense

Awaiting the court's

Final conclusion!

Postpone for time's

Constant intrusion!

Hurray, wait, but

Don't be late!

Ramblings

My mind wanders upon the path between insanity and reality, which may really be insanity. As I travel the creation of myself, trying to see me from outside of me, my mind is questioning itself and an existence. Why is there knowledge of knowing? I have a mind known by my mind.

I realizle exist. Why I exist is in question, with the fact I do exist, why existence around me exists, and how do I affect my existence, and the existence I exist in.

Obviously the existence of me cannot be changed, for I exist, without at first realizing I exist, until recently unaware that the creation that surrounds me also controls me because it has impressed its reality upon my existence, for it states all existence is a plastic, unaware piece of machinery keeping the downfall of mankind progressing towards its ultimate... is it possible destruction? Enslavement by a computerized world dealing purely with logic? Or do we have time to reach the understanding of our relationship with the universe?

There is no more value in death than in life. Perhaps there is no death, only eternity.

The inner mind is somewhat distrubed with the reality that exists in a society that does not have the insight to realize its creation as wrong and harmful to its species.

The interwoven belief that man and woman are the superior race of our world is an ego unnecessary to the fact that life truly exists best in harmony with nature. Man's complete belief that he can control nature is the beginning of the downfall.

The relationship between man and man or man and woman, etc., begins each ego trip. Ego, the word, is the creation of man himself, but Ego of man is what man believes is his ego, thus over centuries man finds truth only in man's creation of communication. This man then tells that man what to believe, stating that what is said is truth, truth a creation of man.

The single fact is man believes he is what he is because man told him he was.

The thought process in man is existing without realizing its existence, for thinking is instantaneous but the cause of its being is still unsolved.

The sphere of reality exists in the circle one creates within his existence, although society itself creates forces of involvement.

*

Contemplate, Reality is the fact of the obvious.

Truth is in the obvious assumption there is truth. There is no truth without untruth.

Therefore there is no truth without untruth.

For every action there is a reaction.

For every truth there is untruth.

For every reality there is unreality.

If truth is reality

Every Reality is truth

Every human is truth

Therefore, every human is reality

Ego is the thought of creation of the self,

The I

If we believe ourselves to be separate, we have the preconceived notion of separate existence. But the first mistake is the assumption that we believe we exist as a separate self.

There is no separation.

My Revolution-My Revelation

I started my personal revolution in the 60s, dealing with my anger towards the system that trapped me as a man, a Warrior to be drafted into a military complex.

The 70s were dealing with the wounded Warrior, trying to find myself, my purpose, my center. The 80s continued my evolution within, while coming to terms with my wounded warrior illusions, of the fallen hero, the Patriot who served his country.

The 90s was a time that accelerated my deeping of my inner awareness, while dealing with the outside world of a dysfunctional government system.

2000, saw a shift inward and a new outlook on physical reality—my body.

2002 and beyond has been fatherhood, understanding parenting, raising a child, a time of being comfortable as an old warrior facing the enemy of time, and freeing my spirit for the final frontier of exploration as a spiritual being, of light, love, and forgiveness—Embracing the unknown with joy, truth, and excitement for the next evolution, the next adventure of my soul.

May 2022

Reworded

Poetry of the past blends with the future by imparting words that long ago
Revealed the moments recorded then at that time and its vision of the
Presence which reflects on the future that it is yet to be.

Shaping the statements of a time and view as seen through the lens of a
Radical perception of a wounded warrior, one who through battle has
Seen the struggles of war and peace, in the midst of a government system
Caught in bureaucrats protecting their jobs—place of identity.
Afraid to adjust to the truth, afraid to face it's dysfunction and its inept attitude of importance
Of following rules and regulations that make no sense.

Magic Moments

Perhaps we miss the splendor of each day

By thinking only of the past

Not seeing the beauty of each moment,

As it unfolds in surrender to the sun.

Like a petal that opens as the sun

Shines upon it, filling it with light.

Do we see the light as it fills the day

Like grace upon, a fragment of time

Bestowing its gentle embrace with ease

Each moment unfolds in a ripple of time,

Seconds and minutes blending into

Hours and days with simple the elegance of

Presence.

Listening to Spirit

Listening to Spirit is very important in today's world of chaos, confusion, and climate change. We must listen to our hearts, where spirit will guide us to be better stewards of Mother Earth.

If more of us listen deeply with our hearts, not our minds, we could create peace, we could create the changes necessary to make planet earth a planet of peace, tranquility, and happiness for all.

We must discard the old ways of anger, war, and negative thinking.

Embracing the new ways will take time but we must start now!

By opening your heart center and listening deeply from that place inside you that is quiet and at peace you can hear the Universe vibrating its messages of peace, tranquility, and love. Problems arise because we are moving too fast to truly listen, to be quiet enough to truly feel the heartbeat of Mother Earth. To turn off our ego concepts of more, more, never enough. These are concepts of Superior to others because we are right and others wrong.

Because they are heathens and I am Religious - Spiritual. Because I am a Republican and they a Democrat, because I am white and they are not, because I am a man and they are a Woman, because the list goes on and on.

We must realize our oneness, our sameness—we are humans living, wanting to be free to express ourselves as loving, kind, compassionate humans, wanting a peaceful life, with the essentials—food, water, shelter, and loving family and friends.

Rebel

I am a rebel

My

Soul is free

No one and nothing controls me

My

Spirit is free

I believe in nothing and everything

My

Heart

 And

Love

Are free!

This poem appeared in *WhipFlash Soup* and *Other Spiritual Ingredients*, published in 2007, which was comprised of most of my early poetry from the 70s and 80s.

Love Ya!

If you weren't you

How could I love

The things about you

If you weren't you

Who would I be

In love with

If you weren't you

Then who

Are you?

True love is loving

Things as they

are

Not as they

Could be!

This poem first appeared in *WhipFlash Soup and Other Spiritual Ingredients*.

Children

Like children

Of the Universe

On a constant Merry-Go-Round

With life as a game

And Eternity the answer

We keep tripping

Down the

Path

As we stumble down

The path of life

Spinning circles in the sand

Of time We Forever

Remain on

The

Merry-Go-Round

Of life

Still searching for

The answers

Wandering in

Each moment

Within our mind

Freda

This is a simple poem, you see

Written especially from me

With rhythm of love and elegant grace,
We send this poem with all do haste

To wish Happy Birthday—84

And to say so much more.

For you are a Mother beyond compare

In the eyes of a Daughter who truly cares—

Serena.

So over miles and miles and Ocean waves,

We send you love and warm embrace

And

Hope your day is filled with God's

Eternal Grace!

Golden Arches

Golden arches

Of a

God–like cult

Mc D Burgers are really fine

Secret Sawdust Sauce

The Chemical kind

eat them up

cram them down!

Coffee, sugar,

Chemical Clowns!

A World of Zombies, muddle around!

Organic weirdos, Shoot them down!

Up with Chemical Milkshakes

USDA Approved!

Not fit for human consumption

Does that mean You!

Trademark and registered, too.

Whirl Winds of Change

whirlwinds

In the midst of change

Everything

In motion

Standing still

In the center of

Time!

Overlooking the infinite

Wholeness

Floating endlessly in

Spacewarp

Cracks

Beneath my feet

Cement shifting with age

I am at peace!

74 years of grace.

White hair that was dark brown

In bygone years.

Once

I once saw the sea

I once saw the grass

I once saw the birds

I once saw the trees

Now I see Billboards

Saying

Ecology!

This poem first appeared in *WhipFlash Soup and Other Spiritual Ingredients*

Sweet Remembrance

Thoughts of you

Enter my mind

Like crystal clear

Raindrops

Developing into

A pool

Of beauty

And an

Ocean of Love

Tranquil

And

Silent!

Inspiration of A Lost Generation

Upon the crystal clear

Reality

Flashes the light

A streaking multicolored

Fragment

Of its original beginning

Slowly building, upon itself

A point of Nowhere is reached

The ultimate

is the

Obvious?

The

True

Revolution

Begins

In you!

This poem first appeared in *WhipFlash Soup and Other Spiritual Ingredients*

WHIP FLASH SOUP INTRODUCTION

This introduction was written in 2007, for the Whip Flash Soup collection of writings I was publishing at that time.

This collection of poetry and words were mostly written during the period of 1972-1977. The last few poems are currently 2004-2006, showing a difference in style and composition of the writings.

My hope is to express my deep inner feelings on the journey called life and to share this journey with all that cross my path.

I would like to thank the many people who have touched me on this journey, so many I cannot remember all the names, so to those I have been touched by but who I do not recall, I say thanks, and blessings.

To the following I express my sincere gratitude for your part in my life's journey; my dad Eddie who was the most gentle, kind man I have ever known and who always encouraged me to follow my own path or drumbeat; to my first love; and to all the hip poets I have known.

Now to my daughter Mayah, and her mother, my partner and wife Serena, who has been an inspiration to my creative energies, and who has encouraged me to publish my poetry.

To my dear friend Pat whom I have co-authored two books, and who has been an inspiration as a writer. And to my friend Harvey, a dear soul on my journey who I have played racquetball and tennis with over many years.

To all my friends at the Metaphysical Research Society, Luann, Peggy Sue, & Ronnie: for their support in my work as a Metis Shamanic Practitioner/Healer and writer on the Spiritual Frontier.

BERKLEY 1973

The point between

I lived on the corner of Woolsey in Oakland, C A

Good and Bad limits

which was a few blocks from the Berkley city

Is

Only the social value

I lived there for 3 months, between my college

Of your peers

experiences

GOLDEN CHARIOT

The situation must change true reality

Exists in bliss, the heart

We must live in harmony with the Universe

Or perish from this earth

Nature should not be conquered

But one with us, and us with nature

Time flows upon the graves

Of the past while the golden chariot

Sinks slowly into the

Bay of Reality!

(This poem was written in 1971)

SHIRLEY ANN

One thought of you

Produces love

A feeling I hope to enjoy again!
Understanding

I thank you for helping me understand

A feeling locked away

I hope no longer to

Hide

The

Key!

APPLE TREE

Tall pine trees

Slender tall Redwoods

And

One small apple tree

Stands out in the middle

of

Nowhere

MADNESS

The simple madness

That surrounds me

Is society

The simple insanity

That I live in

Is me!

The simple fantasy

That exists before me

Is reality

74 REVOLUTIONS PER MINUTE

Revolution

Revolution

Revolution

I have committed mine

Have you

Committed yours?

SPIRITUAL RELEASE

Bubba Free,

Lee,

And all their Grace!

Spiritual slavery— what a Space!

Life's the answer to all you

Face!

BUBBLE

The bubble blows bigger

And bigger

Slowly increasing in

Circular size

Until finally it

Bursts!

COBWEB

A spider clinging to the wall

A web he's spun dusty ridden with

Longing fleas of another era

MOUNTAIN THOUGHT

Peace and quiet,

That's the space People's trips Are out of place

Mountain wilderness

Not the civilized

Rat race!

(Autumn 1976, Mendocino County California)

I owned an 80 acre parcel of land backing up to the National Forest, which I was homesteading.

10 MINUTES FROM NOWHERE

A small little town that

Calmly goes on its way

A lovely ?? and her child

Walk swiftly downtown

With the freshness of

A newborn day

The trees waving

In joy

(Dillon Beach, California, 1974, Summer)

THE ILLUSIONS OF THE WORLD

As time slowly sails by…….

Bankers, Lawyers,

And Politicians too

Live their dreams,

As Reality

The Zen Monk

Sits silently

The river flows endlessly!

TRANQUILITY

My mind endlessly wanders

Thoughts and patterns

Changing instantly

I look at the yellow green grass

Growing in the we ridden

Environment

Sometimes its Blank

Seemingly as empty

As the air!

SINSEMILLA ROCKS MY SOUL

I love you sweet momma

When you stone that way

I love sweet momma

What can I say ?

I love you sweet momma

When you pour out those resins

Day by day

I love you sweet momma

Sinsemilla!

You're here to stay!

I love you sweet momma

And there's no more to say!

STONED

A freaked out moment

In time

When reality

Hits you on

The last

Toke!

(The above poems were written during a time of dealing with my PTSD from the army and trying to cope with life as a wounded warrior. I have since given up on using such drugs to calm my nerves and ease my physical pain from military injuries suffered while serving my country) I am a lifetime member of Vietnam Veterans of America, and a certified Veterans Peer Corp Mentor, helping other Veterans deal with their disabilities and traumas related to War. I served in the army in 1969 and 1970, as a Medic.

GARDEN

Back to the garden

To grow sweet daisies

And weeds

Back to the hills

And

Redwood trees

Back to classical

Music and my Poetry!

(Written 1974 upon leaving Urban America)

THE ROOM

The green room looks drab

But not barren

A spice of life

In each piece of furniture

Yet it's still a lonely room T

hat's green!

(a room I rented for a summer in Occidental, California, 1974)

PASSING BY

Tomorrow lingers overhead

As today passes by

Almost unnoticed

Like

A soft summer shower

That comes and goes

Within raindrops

Of a moment!

40 STEPS TO THE LEFT

Time

Is always right,

When endless space

Is

Directly in front

Of

You!

ONE DAY IN MY LIFE

As I sit with memories of the past

And visions of the future

All within a single moment

Sly and the Family stone at Stanford University

The Rolling Stones, Winterland! Woodstock-2,

A future fantasy?

Love, Hate, and Reality!

PRIMAL MADNESS

Upon a lonely night

Fear

Sits among us

We

Watch it play with our minds

Like children we are captured!

WILLIAM TELL OVERTURE

A lonely moment slips

Into a sunny day

On a rain - filled night

Turns foggy

A stillness fills

The air with freshness

And the flowers once

Again open to the

Joyous light.

RIDICULOUS

Simple creation

Of reality

Existence of love in heart

Right is wrong

There is no right

There is no wrong

Only existence of the

Moment

We only exist at this present

Moment!

In time

Which we say exists!

BULLSHIT

I could write a twenty-two

Page analysis

On the structure

Of words in relationship

To structured Communication

Instead

I write these words

Bullshit!

Donkeys!

And people!

MY

My writing is funny

My writing is a joke

I write out of stupidity

My writing is nowhere

I write out of madness

My writing is isane

My writing is smoke

I write out of fear

My writing won't stop!

MARY SUE AND CINDY TOO

I sit here

With thoughts

Of coming and going

Wondering where I'm at

Between the Blues and Soul

My

Head is caught up in

Rock n Roll

Swinging underneath the

Apple tree

Just sweet

Mary Sue and

Cindy too

(one sunny day in the park, 1974)

LOVE YA

If you weren't you

How could I love

The things about you

If you weren't you

Who would i be

In love with

If you weren't you

Then who

Are you

True love is loving

Things as they

Are

Not as they

Could be!

RADICAL

REALIZATIONS

Radical Realization,

Spiritual Enlightenment,

Holy Spirit,

Grace,

The total awareness of man

Living in the world

Known as reality

That which

Is!

BLACK RYE

Black rye

Behind the

Bread box

Turning stale

Since I have nothing to

Write

I'll stop

MEDITATE!

SWING SLOWLY

Swinging slowly clock like

Waves of death ridden

Stones

Tortured in realism

Of moments

Happening

Endlessly

Forever!

AFTER THE MORNING

After the morning

Fog clears the valley

The little gold and white

 trimmed house shines brightly

In the afternoon sun.

Wind whistles throughout

The community

Three hundred

Harmonious human beings

(Occidental-Freestone, Sonoma County, California, 1974)

MOMENTS NOTICE

Little roses in bloom

On the hillside,

The sun shines slowly

With gentleness

On the hillside

Endowing each

Petal

With

Life Full Love!

WOMEN

Women are my fancy

With all I wish to be

Yet one is on my mind

Not a constant changing

Scene!

(La Honda, Big Sur, California, 1973)

SUDDENLY

Suddenly the earth is free

Hatred has broken loose

And hell is upon the earth

Fire is destroying the beauty

And chaos is amongst us

Evil is waiting for the final Moment

Man has fallen to his knees

And then She appears

With only a word it happens

Suddenly the Earth is free!

TOGETHER

United in cause

And solve the problem

By

Creating the solution

Which

Gives the answer

To the question!

ONE DAY IN 74

I can condone

My reality

Work ethic !

= causes frustration reaction !

Subjective Classification

must fit within limits

Consuming Space Human reality

Occidental Happening

A blue and white old truck

Pulled into the dead end street

Of the small tourist town !

Changing clothes

To become a new identity

Acceptable to

Who !

(the couple climbed out of the truck and went and ate dinner in the fancy restaurant down the street, Occidental, California Summer, 1974)

BLISS IS BEFORE ME

We cause all frustrations

Knowledge is Narcissus

Ego, psychologically unnecessary

To exist, in harmony

With planet Earth !

REALITY

Enjoy the present now

For it exists !

Tomorrow is a

Word !

ANSWER ME

The evolution, revolution

The entering of the 4th Dimension

Time, Space, Eternity, and Reality

4th Dimensional Space Revolution

Whispering thought across your

Mind

The third book will

Be on Crime !

UNNOTICED

The morning's sunlight

Warms slowly

Rumbling echoes of the

Trucks slipping by

Birds chirping cheerfully

From the dew covered pine trees

A simple quiet morning

Unnoticed ?

G.I. BLUES

A VietNam Era

Of time been done

A Veterans fate

Of the Corporate ones

A money shortage, Inflation fund

The G.I. lost

Who has won ?

(written while waiting in a Veterans Administration office-1975)

NO NAME

A prison like view

With bar

Yet it's a picture window

In middle America

It's the hip new look

That's clean and cold

Plastic gardens

All in a row !

(driving through San Francisco, California)

KATHLEEN

A simple sweet innocent smile

A darling daughter syndrome

Kathleen

The fresh look of a college student

Being reborn into childhood

A woman she shall be !

FRIENDSHIP

A poem of friendships' might

To reach the heavens , as spirits unite,

Across the water, a sky so bright,

Filled with love and delight.

For friendships form from golden light

And hearts that open to the night

To share the mysteries of each other's right

To walk the path of God's delight

Make friendships special in my sight.

COURTROOM DRAMA

A serious silence

Questions, and answers

Dice and Dominos

Chess games plays

Legal locks

Truth the key

Judge is God- God is Judge?

Time schedule

Weighing balance

Technical problems,

Code book solutions

MIDDLE AGE SPREAD

40 frustrations with aging time!

Middle age spread!

Balding gray spots on my head

On surfer images and hippy dreams !

Aging radical with capitalist seams

Wearing suits of corruption for

Pension extreme !

TIME CONTROL
Remembered

Within these hallowed halls of justice

We prepare the motion mix

To play the legal game in action !

Time sits still in all its glory, Suspended by the Judge's order,

Fix the time and the date to reappear

Before the bench

Lawyers, Judges, and the Clerks

Work in details and perfection

But final say can be rendered Only by code books silent Surrender

Accept the fate

Of rules and regulations,

Society's answer to the equation !

Control is but just an illusion of confusion!

WOW!

Speed bound haste

Rushing to class

Early arrival

Moments wait

Changes coming

Magic works

education, learning, growing

Inner light, hearts delight, God's sight

Caught in between

Fire and Flame

Love is crazy

Minds outright

Joy and pleasure, pain and hate

Two worlds apart, Endless trap

Caught in moments far apart

Heart surrender

To tear apart

Longing joys, singing sorrows,

Love today

Gone tomorrow

BOOGIE

Boogie on down to the promised land

I got a plan

To tell the Man

A united plan For the land

I've got the word

I've got the way

Give peace a chance

Make it your dance

Love all the people

Throw hate away!

Open up your heart to a new and brighter day!

EACH DAY

Each day is an opportunity to share joy, light, and wisdom. Another day unfolds in grand splendor.

The joy and light and wisdom we carry within us must be shared each day for every day is our awakening of our soul's purpose to be, that joy, that light.

With each breath we take in, the divine fills us with air to survive, to sustain us. Each released breath is a release of the joy within us to the world.

So let us express from our hearts the fantastic joy to be alive, to be living in this incredible time of planetary change.

I am blessed to be able to express my delight at living during this time of great change by embracing the joy of each moment, as I sense it unfolding with each breath.

Each step I take is a step forward on my path, a path that is filled with a multidimensional level of learning, challenges, and opportunities.

I walk a Spirit–lead path that travels through a lower world, a middle world, and an upper world, each world with its own wonder and delight.

RAINY MAY DAY

The droplets fall upon the spring flowers, dancing with delight as each droplet bursts into a puddle of moist earth.

A sigh of relief is felt as the air sparkles with freshness.

The sun shines through the mist of rain, rainbow light scatters across the rain soaked soil, as life itself explodes in awe of nature's energy.

The sky thunders, as clouds pass overhead, lightning flashes across the horizons, the storm has arrived in full fury to the dance of water pouring in streams of might.

SEATTLE SCENE 22

Where it rains and is cloudy most days,
Where it's green and lush rainforests
Meet skyscrapers, Space needle, and
Chihuly glass masterpieces
Where computer programs mingle with
Homeless people, a mist of foggy vapors
Underground tours with insights of the past
That's hidden in the weaving of history,
A tale of past not so well known
A city of delight, a city of insights, a
City of music, a city of seahawks flying
Over head
Pike's market alive with people, sellers,
Buyers, and lookers
Cascade wonders, and mountains beyond
Seattle City by the sea.

Afterthoughts- Ending Musings

Well it summer 2023, Scotland and I am settling into some new routines, bundling up more with layers, as the weather changes every few hours, and the winds is constant. The sea is not far away a north sea of beauty. My time is now exploring my surroundings, feeling village life, walking to the town square, to the small shops, the friendly people a slow pace of life. One where I can smell the roses in my front yard, red,orange, pink, yellow. Sipping a cup of earl grey tea, while I type on this laptop at my desk in a room that is cozy. I want to thank my partner Serena for her support and our child River for the cover design.

Well it's July 2024, and I am just getting around to publishing these poems. I have been in Scotland now over a full year, and the pace of the small town of Lossiemouth, is finally settling within me, and I feel like I am truly finding my nitch, my place, my new rhythm.

I believe I will continue to write the rest of my Adult life, for it allows the kid in me to express it self, and to play with words, feelings, and fantasies that come through my mind/brain. Some of my writing is like flashes of insights, thoughts or twisted ideas that pop into my thoughts.

I am so affected by the environment and people around me that I feel a pulsating vibration of the Spirits around me the Fairies, elves,and animals, especially the cat Twinkle Toes, for she is an incredible furry bundle of joy and loves for me to do Reiki on her and to pet her at least five

times a day.

My walks to the beach are an inspirational element of my current writing agenda, and require I allow the sea to speak to me, for the sand to go between my toes (only on warm days), and for the wind to blow ideas, thoughts, and imagination into my face.

So to all of you who read this manuscript, I hope it gives you some laughs, some sparks of inspiration, and a little insight into my world, my reality as I express it through these written words , a collection of my writings unedited and raw. Enjoy, and if you have any feedback , I would love hear from you, send me an email, comment on Facebook, Instagram, or any social media platform I have a page.

Other books I have authored or contributed to:

Crystal Reiki Workbook, with author Lyncara Aria Stewart

Crystaline Reiki

Crystal and Gemstone Healing

Medical Intuition Handbook

Medical Intuition and Muscle Testing, with Author Pat Doughtery, D.C.

Life Changing Lessons from an Elder: Learning the Metis Medicine Ways, co-authored with Charles Edwards, PhD

Sound Healing with Tuning Forks

Advance Sound Healing with Tuning Forks

Whipflash Soup & Other Spiritual Ingredients (Poetry)

Musings: written works/poetry/philosophy

Workbook learning to Channel

Vibrational Yoga: Sacred Sound and Movement

Bits and Pieces of Nonsense (poetry)

Animal Medical Intuition, with author Lyncara Aria Stewart

Pain Relief with Tuning Forks

Cellphone Forgotten

I forgot my cell phone, Am I lost without it?

Or is it a freedom to think

To not be connected to a constant beep, beep if there is

A message or a phone that rings with sales calls

Promoting an agenda

Should I be upset, at myself, Forgetting the phone

Or realize it is Divine Intervention, Awaking me to silence, a shift from Staring at a screen in a daze of Conformity.

What else might I see if

Just looking at my surroundings

The beauty of the day

The stars at night

So in forgetting my cell phone am I Bad, sad, or glad?

A matter of perception, I might say.

A time to write a poem or essay, a time to
Think and ponder Without technology to Bother!
A time to reflect within.

Dad Day 22

Waking up alone, on Father's day, the silence of the house fills me

Only to be broken by the cat's meow, for attention and food

A remembrance of a daughter, a wife far away in Scotland,

Visiting her own dad, one last time.

Moments of stillness, quiet, as I awaken to this special day,

The rain lightly falling on the flowers, as I watch, looking through

The window, drinking my morning tea, remembering

Times past, the joy of Fatherhood.

Waiting to see my daughter arrive soon, to embrace me, To smile at me, to reflect back at me memories of her Childhood.

Child of Rhyme

As I look at him/her,
I see myself, my wife
Looking back at me!
I see my daughter/son
A person they be!
A collection of thoughts, ideas, In the person I see!
The young, the old, the inbetween,
Captured in front of me!
The creation of a person is like the
Seed that becomes a tree!

I wrote this prose during a time of sorting out my feelings and deepening my understanding of what my child needs, and them finding out where they felt they fit within the world.

Friendship

When people embrace
Each other in mutual fun
Support each other
In trauma and tragedy
With hugs and insights
When people accept the
Faults of others, as
Part of life's treasure
When moments
Of laughter
Stir the
Feelings of love
And
Moments of sadness
Stir
Feelings of compassion
We open our hearts in
Friendship to
Those we align as
Chosen family
Lineage not required.
Missing You Missing You
Words can not express the
Feeling of loneliness, of
Missing Your Wife,
Your partner,
Your spiritual Muse
The absence of your Presence
Fills the mind with thoughts,
With longings to

> Embrace you
> To touch your soul essence
> Emptiness fills the time
> We normally share together
> A void of space that
> Lingers in thoughts, rituals
> And restless sleep
> With dreams interrupted
> Spells and visions
> Consume the moments
> Lost in time
> Missing you is out of
> Rhyme or Reason !
> Aging Elderhood-2022

This year I turn 75, three quarters of a century and I realize I am as some friends say in the final third of my life (assuming I live to be a hundred, although I am shooting for 120). Yet I still have many more books to write, stories to tell, apprentices and students to mentor, workshops to teach, and ceremonies to perform.

My life is full, but now I take more time to meditate, contemplate, and just be present. I spent my childhood learning—observing the ways to become an adult in society, although I was not ready until I was 25, to even consider myself an adult.

As an adult I continue to work to form my persona, identity.

Then at 55 I hit a milestone, that had me grow up: I became a Father, and an Elder in the local Wolf Clan, and settled into more teaching, writing articles and asking myself what is the meaning of life. What gifts am I here to give?

Have I given them?

What more do I need to do?

I realized I need to share my knowledge more (hence writing books) and continue to learn more wisdom from the ancient ways of my ancestors.

To dig deeper into my celtic roots, to understand my lineage from my Mother's & Father's family trees.To piece together the puzzle of my mixture of European heritage and my Native American heritage. To see how it composts into the person I am today.

Today I am a mixture of a mother who was born of parents of English and German bloodline and of my father who was of French and Cherokee descent.

So the combination of their bloodlines created me, a mixture of various cultures and backgrounds. So I spent part of my adulthood exploring my roots, my bloodline.

This began the understanding that I was Metis, as my mentor Dale Three Feathers would call me, he said Metis meant a mixed bloodline and culture.

Dale Three Feathers encouraged me to find my roots, my connection to the cultures my parents knew as they were growing up in the world. This quest to search my ancestral lineage led me to study many cultures beyond my own. To understand the common traits and beliefs all cultures have in dealing with the world and surviving with dignity and purpose.

My quest continues, however. I have collected a lot of knowledge which I share with my apprentices and students. I feel it is important for everyone to have a deep understanding of their heritage and family lineage, so as to connect with their roots and to learn the ancient ways their forebears used to survive and live during their times on planet earth.

So how does this affect aging?

Well I think if we better understand our roots, where we came from, we could age more gracefully, more fully, and also pass on this information to our children and grandchildren. Aging well depends upon our acceptance of ourselves as Elders (holders of wisdom) and realizing it's another step in the process of living.

This was written during the summer of 2022 at the end of June a few months before my birthday in September. I feel grateful I have survived this long in human form.

Writings

My writings are a way for me to reflect on my journey, to take note of the bumps, the ups, the downs, and the mundane moments I experience in this human form as Charles.

I enjoy the act of writing and for the most part still write these words in longhand on paper and then type them on to the computer as a word doc, sometimes with minor changes.

My writings are my thoughts, ideas, feelings, and inspirations that come to me, at the beginning of the day, middle of the day, or end of the day, even occasionally in the middle of the night so I have to get up from sleep to compose the words running through my mind.

I find inspiration in my quiet time, my time before social interaction with others. I also get inspiration from my daughter—Mayah—as she is filled with questions, thoughts, and creative energy that is catching. There is also the encouragement of my wife Serena to go deeper within, to go beyond my limitations, beyond the victim triangle, to be present and face my demons, my darkness, my limitations.

To boldly go forward with conscious awareness.

To explore the depths of my soul and to feel the sensations of life. To live fully in the present yet learn from the past.

To accept my inner child and support its feelings in creating the person I am now.

With the support of my daughter and wife, I feel I am making progress towards revealing my true self, so that I may grow, evolve, and become conscious of my actions, reactions, and habit patterns I have created so far on this life's journey.

How remarkable it is that I have survived the educational system, the military service, and being a wounded warrior in a crazy world that ignores the emotional costs of living a life of truth, while dealing with a political system filled with corruption by greed and power hungry people only interested in serving themselves, not in serving the people.

At least, this is my perspective on the matter.

This was written during the year 2022, June.

Free The Word

So I see the signs, commercials with the word Free used, But is it truly free?

The definition of Free is; Free (verb) enjoying personal rights

Or liability as a person not in salvery.

But what I am talking about is the misuse of the word Free

Free in today's terms seems to be with a condition.

Free is you/me buying this or that, then it's free

And the one that really is laughable to me is; Free with purchase.

So really the word Free is overused.

How can anything be free if you have to spend money?

Which brings me to the expanded word, Freedom

Freedom, the state of being free

Are any of us truly free?

And what is Freedom, a word that means,

The condition or right of being able to do, say, think, etc.

So do we have Freedom or is Freedom conditional?

We are in a state of freedom as long as we allow others

To Be Free.

So freedom is for everyone, not a select group of people

Or is freedom bought with money?

The more money you have the freer you are?

Questions for us to answer!

Old Age

Age is a state of mind, however the body does show signs of age. So, my mind may feel or think it's thirty, but my body is seventy-five. I have wisdom, I have bumps and bruises, because I have emotional turmoil over years of ignoring what I truly feel.

My mind may reach a state of peace, but my mind might hold anger over what is still held on too. Release the anger, release the stress—look in the mirror at your own distress.

With time we see gray hair and baldness creep in, a lack of facing facts will soon set in, to rhythm this open with my pin.

Wine Wisdom? Intoxicate State.

To have a taste of Syrah, can make a palate go Hurrah!

A mixed blend can bless you out with a feeling of Aha!

A red so pure is truly bliss and takes you to a place of Aha!

But most of all the wine can take the grape of Ya!

And make you desire more

So drink up to taste your last Aha!

For drinking wine can be the best if you know it's your last hurrah!

This poem was composed while drinking a T-3 Blend from Townsend Winery in July 20022, after watching a play that was incredible. I was blessed with a good bottle of wine and watching a play with my child on a warm summer afternoon in Spokane, WA. USA.

Anniversary 2022

I celebrate this special day, our marriage, our milestone of years together as a couple, a partnership of mutual support, of parenting our daughter, of allowing each other to grow as people to deepen our spiritual connection to Source. This day marks another year of love, embracing our human development, our expanded awareness. Although we are apart on this special day, in our hearts, our spirit, we are united in our commitment to each other.

Happy Anniversary Serena, My Beloved

Charles

Creating a life that reflects your values and satisfies your soul is a rare achievement.

"In a culture that relentlessly promotes Avarie and access as the good life, a person happy doing one's on work is usually considered an eccentric, if not a subversive".

   - Bill Watterson

I have always lived an eccentric life, walking my own path, to the beat of my own drum, listening to Spirit, following my heart, and I am content!

   - Charles Lightwalker

Death

Death for those dying is a release of the body

Death for those of us associated with the Dying person are

Grief, sadness, confusion, denial, and a going within looking at Our own mortality.

Death is a ceasing of function on the human plane of existence, A letting go of the physical form–a body–yet allowing the soul to

Move interdimensionally to another level of awareness, a

Different place of consciousness, that exists beyond our Three

Dimensional existence, a place not describable compared to our current level of awareness.

Sayings- Quips

I like saying, quotes, and quips, etc.

However, some sayings are quite odd

One example:

Time is Money

You can have all the money of a Billionaire, but you can't buy

Time

The universe has more time than money, why people use this term is

Sad, as the most important things in life

Cannot be bought with money like

Love, Compassion, Gratitude, and more. Another is:

Money is Evil

Perhaps the worship, or hoarding of money can have its negative

impacts on people, but money itself is not evil

How one spends or uses money possibly is

Besides money itself is a creation people made up! Money itself only has the value the government gives it.

Money is a creation of society, a way to barter for goods or services

Nothing more.

Let's get back to basics, loving one another, helping one another

Stop the competitive nature that society put forth as normal

What is normal is love, compassion, and caring for others.

Tarot Card reading by River, July 2022 (her first time)

Me represented by- the Magician

Person at current time of reading, King of cups, representing a fair man

Next, six of swords, Obstacles feeling lost Five of swords, Represents my ideals-wants Four of swords, solitude retreat

Moving out of, six of wands -Moving away from old expectations

Moving into, the seen, Contempt

Attitude toward self, the Hermit, Vulcan like structure routine

My family, High Priestess, surface knowledge of family

Hope and fears, eight of Swords, afraid something disquiets me

Future, Judgement, Simplicity – deliberation

Flashes of My Life

I have decided to include bits and pieces of my life's adventure into these musings of writings (more are in my autobiography). They are snippets of different times in my journey, that are different parts of me that make the whole of who I am today.

We all have various stages of life experience that mold us into the person we are now as of this writing. These moments capture the person I was when I experienced them and I believe each experience builds an awareness of our potential to become more engaged in life as a human being having a spiritual experience while in a body. Each of these flasheswere the building blocks of my journey, my connection to Spirit which has been with me my entire life. I hope you enjoy these flashes of my life.

Charles–July–2022

My first flash was when I was a year old or so. I was crawling around trying to stand up to try and walk. I was in the garage with my dad and I tried standing up by leaning on an old door that was leaning against the wall. As I got up the door shifted and fell toward me, knocking me back onto the concrete floor with the door coming down on my head. I saw flashes of light and my head started to hurt and swelled up. I went out of my body for a moment or so–I was in a state of surreal sensations. Part of this memory came to me during a hypnosis session, and parts were told to me by my parents.

My next flash was at age 12: My mother's death was another surreal experience–I can still remember quite clearly seeing my mother in spirit. After her passing, one of these times being when I was at her funeral, she sat next to me as the Priest and others spoke about her. All her family was there to say Goodbye. She smiled at me and looked at peace. She whispered "remember what I taught you. I'll come to your dreams to teach you more. It was my time to go, take care of your Dad.

I have finished my mission on earth to raise you to this age of a young man, now it is your my fathers turn. If you need to talk to me get quiet, go within, use the meditation and intuitive abilities you have to connect with my spirit."

These experiences continued for a number of years, especially at night. One time I had a dream that I could enhance my intuitive abilities to look at people and their auras, the color around them that showed me their moods. So then I started seeing them in real life. I also dreamt that I needed to remember we all have spirit guides and angels around us that can help us if we ask and if we pay attention to listening with our heart.

There are other experiences where listening to spirit guides or angels have saved my life or made me aware of the importance of listening from my heart. Sometimes I would get strong sensations, feelings, and flashes of my mother talking: saying "listen. Be quiet for a moment."

I am 16 walking home alone from a football game I had watched at my high school. I reached a point where I could take two different paths home. One was through a neighborhood and the other was walking along the railroad tracks for a distance and then turning down a street towards my home. I have a sensation that I need to be quiet and listen to my inner guidance. I look in each direction.The neighborhood seems strange and foreboding. The railroad track seemed light, peaceful, and smooth. So, I went the way of the railroad tracks, which seemed odd only in that that way was darker–fewer street lights–but was a pleasant walk. Then the next day I discovered that the neighborhood I would have walked through had been home to a huge gang fight where one person was killed and several injured.

 This next incident happened when I was eighteen. I was in my car driving on a mountain road that weaved around itself with no way to see around the corners as you were approaching them. Suddenly, I hear a voice say "pull in closer to the curb now." I did that and within a moment a car came around the corner going very fast and on my side of the road. If I had remained where I was, I would have been hit head on.

Now I am in the army. I am twenty years old. I am in the barracks with a group of trainees, preparing for be, when all of a sudden we hear a lot of noise from the upstairs group of trainees. A few of us decide to go see what is going on and as I turn the corner to go up the stairs I hear "stop. Don't go up the stairs". I ignore the voice and a few moments later a garbage can comes hurling down the stairs at me and another guy, knocking us backwards into others. There is pain and blood coming from my knee where the garbage can had hit me and the other guy's leg is bleeding as well. So I was off to the hospital, on crutches for a month, and was reminded of why I usually listen to my inner voice.

I was in a class with a group of trainees taking tests. One of the Instructors asked this question: "Have any of you ever see a ghost or spirit"? A voice said to raise my hand, so I did, and then I was asked to follow the other instructor to another room for other tests. This led to some interesting experiences with a group of army people studying the paranormal, intuition, and out of body experiences. all classified information of course.

Some of my work was doing remote viewing behind "enemy lines".

More of my military experiences will be included in another book, I am currently writing with Professor Charles Edwards, PhD.

More Writings- More Written work

Now back to some more poetry and thoughts, I am a writer of thoughts, poetry, philosophy, and random ideas that appear in my mind, I love to write, especially about healing modalities I have studied, taught, and in some cases mastered the healing art of various modalities, such was the case with sound healing with tuning forks, I found the scientific calibrated tuning forks to be fascinating, and that vibration was all around us, in us, and moving through us daily. Also my research into Reiki, has taken me into so many Reiki modalities that I have lost count as to how many now I have studies and masters over the years, first with Usui Reiki, Tibetan Reiki to Holy Fire and Angelic Reiki, each with their own feeling, their own transmission of energies that can affect the body, raise one's vibration , and produce dramatic healing experiences. I have found that combining Reiki with other healing modalities, can provide a deeper, richer experience. I completely enjoyed doing research on using Reiki before Chiropractic treatments, working with Dr. Pat Doughtery was an exhilarating experience and fun, getting the feedback we did during the experiments with doing the Reiki before the treatments, after the treatments, and how each way had its own feeling and dynamic relationship to the adjustment process. Putting all the data into a format that became a book was insightful for me in how to present this material in such as way as to create a story about how two healers came together to mix healing modalities in such away that it proved beneficial to the person receiving the treatment, and how it improved the treatment itself, and how it even affect the two healers, each performing their own part of the process. Quantum Healing: the Synergy of Chiropractic and Reiki. This collaboration led me to devel more deeply into Reiki, and to combine Reiki, with Crystals, Tuning Forks, Intuitive Emotional release. It lead me to study different forms of Reiki,Holy Fire, Angelic, Alchemy

Reiki, Atlantean Reiki, Celtic Reiki, Divine Light Reiki, Dolphin Heart Reiki, Medicine Reiki, and many other Reiki's It also lead me to write Crystaline Reiki, and to write a book with Lyncara Aria Stewart, Reiki Master Teacher called Crystal Reiki Workbook. I continue to study and learn more about healing at every opportunity, and now that I am in Scotland new opportunities are opening up to expand my knowledge of healing.I have also revised my crystal and stone booklets into one book, with all the booklets combined.Since moving to scotland, I have been motivated to finish up my book projects and new consider new book ideas.I am going to redo

my Medical Intuition certification program and adapt it to UK standards, and do a book with Lyncara on Animal Medical Intuition, and included material from my training as an Animal Reiki Master Teacher training, with Lyncara's animal communication material.

I just feel very motivated to learn more, teach more and do more writing.

www.ingramcontent.com/pod-product-compliance
Lightning Source LLC
Chambersburg PA
CBHW081618100526
44590CB00021B/3488